Rosella Vantaggi

MANTUA

AND HER ART TREASURES

HONESTO OCIO   POST·LABORES   AD·REPARANDAM

Published and printed by

NARNI - TERNI

Sole Distributor

OREMPULLER
Fotoedizioni - Trento
www.orempuller.com

MANTUA

To the tourist who comes here for the first time, Mantua looks like lying in an almost unreal and magic atmosphere, surrounded as it is by wates and often wrapped in a silver veil of mist, from which its two towers and belfries stand out.

The town rose on two islets made of the silts of the Mincio. It is washed on three sides by the river, which forms the Upper Lake to north-west, the Middle Lake to noth-east, and the Lower Lake to the east. A fourth lake, the Paiolo, got silted up at the end of the 18th century.

All around the town, beyond the loop surrounding the built-up area, extends a large and fertile plain, where the silence reigns among the polars, which rise high towards the sky, as if they tried to compete with the bell-towers of the numerous villages of this area. Only towards the north one sees the mild slopes of the hills, which constitute the morainic amphitheatre of Garda. From those hills one can see the shining blue waters of the Benoco and the outlines of the high mountains forming its wonderful scenery.

In this plain the poetry of its tradition, dating back to centuries ago, but still living today, and the monotonous peace of country life pervading the humble and patient work of the fields with a mystical solemnity, sharpen the sensibility of the spirit. And it was from the contemplation « of this deep sweetness of a green-coloured land-scape » that Virgil's Georgics were born. Virgil is the great Mantuan, the poet of the Roman Empire, who mainly sang the poetry of the land, strictly connected to the quiet vision of his native fields and his love of Italy.

Right in the centre of that plain, among the loops and ponds formed by the Mincio and constituting a very good natural defence, rose the first prehistorical village, dating back probably to 2000 B.C. From it, around the year 1000, the Etruscan town developed. Mantua kept, for along time, the memory of a mythical founder, the hero Oenus, and of a male deity, Mantus, to whom the founder dedicated the town. Later on, the Romans confused him with Mantios, the Greek diviner, daughter of the Homeric Tiresias.

Then the town was occupied by the Gauls and by the Romans. In a not well known age, perhaps in the 3d or 4th century, Christianity spread in Mantua, as the tradition concerning St. Longinus and the cult of the relics of Christ's Blood, now kept in the Basilica of St. Andrew, clearly show.

After the fall of the empire, the town was invaded by barbarians and by the Goths, Byzantines, Longobards and Franks. Around the year 1000 A.D., Mantua became part of the feuds of the Attoni family, called Canossa, whose last representative was the Countess Mathilda (1046-1115). After her death, Mantua became a free town and strenously defended its freedom against the imperial forces in the 12th and 13th centuries. Then its territory became larger, magnificent monuments were built, among which the Broletto Palace and the Palace of Reason, the marshes of the Mincio were reclaimed by Alberto Pitentino, walls were built around the town.

During the fights between the Guelphs and the Ghibellines, Pinamonte Bonacolsi seized power in 1273, and his family ruled Mantua for more than a century, making it more prosperous and artistically beautiful. At that time were built the Bonacolsi Palace, the Captains' Palace, the « Arengario », the Magna Domus and the churches of Gradaro and St. Francis, which gave the town its peculiar medieval look. We don't have here, however, the characteristic medieval net of narrow streets, forming a sort of stronghold, but large spaces. And it is very pleasant to take shelter from the hot sun of the Lower Po Valley, in the shade of its ruins, though they remind us of terrible civil wars and massacres.

In 1323, at the death of Rinaldo, called Passerino, killed during a revolt fomented by the Gonzaga family, the rule of the Bonacolsi family came to an end, and that of the Gonzaga began with Luigi, the People's Captain and the forefather of this famous family.

Under the Gonzaga family, whose members were made marquises by the Emperor Sigismund, and dukes in 1530 by Charles V, Mantua became the capital town of an important State and went through a period of military glory and artistic splendour, which lasted about four centuries. It was during this period that its largest buildings, true masterpieces of art and magnificence, were built. They were St. George's Castle and the Sanctuary of the Graces. Famous men, such as Ariosto, Tasso, Correggio, Tiziano and Cellini frequented the court of the Gonzaga. Pisanello and Vittorino of Feltre, too, called by Gianfranco Gonzaga, came to Mantua. Vittorino founded here the renowned humanistic school of Ca' Zoiosa (Giocosa).

Under Ludovico II, Mantua, which had still a Gothic look, accepted the new Renaissance art, giving hospitality to Brunelleschi, Fancelli, Alberti, Laurana, Mantegna, Poliziano. Leon Battista Alberti and Andrea Mantegna, however, particularly influenced the artistic life of Mantua. Then, after the prosperous years, when Isabella of Este corresponded with the greatest artists and writers of Italy, a general decline began with the long reign of Giulio Romano. Having already built the so called Tea Palace, he rearranged the city-plan of Mantua, leaving traces of his work practically in every square and building of the town.

In the mean time, the rule of the Gonzaga family extended to Monferrato, too, reaching so the apex of its economical and political prosperity, while at the borders of their dukedom various autonomous territories were created under the rule of the side branches of the family.

In 1627 the main line of the Gonzaga family came to an end and so the town slowly declined. Succession wars, the sack of the imperial forces and the pestilence made the situation worse and worse. In 1707, when the last descendant of the family was deposed, Mantua passed under the Austrian rule.

During this century the town again went through a period of artistic splendour. It was then that the dome of St. Andrew's, the Scientific Theatre and the solemn and majestic Sordi, D'Arco, Valenti, Corriani and Canossa Palaces were built.

Having been besieged by Napoleon, after various vicissitudes, Mantua passed again under the Austrians in 1814, so becoming one of the strongholds of the famous « Quadrilatero » (quadrilateral). In spite of the oppressive rule of the Austrians, the liberal ideals spread among the people, and in the years 1851-1855, with the sacrifice of the Martyrs of Belfiore, the town wrote one of its most beautiful and glorious pages of the Italian « Risorgimento ».

In 1866 Mantua was annexed to the Italian State. Today it is a very busy town, often crowded with many tourists. The industrial area, situated beyond the lakes and surrounded by poplars, is extending more and more. The trading and agricultural activities of three prosperous regions, namely Lombardia, Veneto and Emilia, converge into this town, and even ways of saying used in all these three areas influence its dialect.

Yet, the modern and busy Mantua of today has kept all its variously fascinating aspects of its past, in spite of all the vicissitudes of its history and the many changes it went through.

◄ On the preceding big plate, there is a very suggestive picture of the Mantuan landscape: still waters with grey and soft reflections, long lines of green and silver poplars, softened lights, poetic sunsets, nights with twinkling stars, waters just rippled by mild breezes on the lakes surrounding the town.

SPARAFUCILE'S HOUSE – This small building, stiuated at the end of St. George's Bridge, dividing the Middle Lake from the Lower Lake, is so called after the well known character of Verdi's Rigoletto. It is one of the many towers built to defend the outside city-walls. Its true name is « Rocchetta di San Giorgio ».

St. George's Castle

Together with the Ducal Palace and the Basilica of St. Barbara, St. George's Castle is part of the Gonzaga Palace, which is not a single building, but includes many buildings dating back to various periods, and connected one to the other by inside passages and situated on a large area included between Sordello Square and the lake. In order to have an idea of the vastity of this palace, one has to know that it includes 500 rooms, some of which are very large halls, and 15 open-air areas, namely courtyards, gardens and squares.

The inside halls, thanks to their beauty and variety and the great number of very valuable works of art kept in them, bear witness to the splendour of the Gongaza court. St. George's Castle, built at the end of the 14th century by order of Francis I Gonzaga, is one of the best examples of the military architecture of Bartolino of Novara. It was built for military purposes, but in the second half of the 15th century Ludovico II Gonzaga decided to leave the Old Court and to live there with his wife Barbara Hohenzollern of Brandeburg. For this reason the castle was rearranged and decorated by two artists, Andrea Mantegna and the architect and sculptor Luca Fancelli, who had the task of transforming the severe fortress into a comfortable and magnificent house.

Outwardly, the building keeps the essential elements of the beautiful square structure conceived by Bartolino for its original function.

In the interior, in the centre of the building, there is the Courtyard, surrounded on three sides by porticoes, of which the oldest one is that on the north side, while the other two were added in 1472 by Luca Fancelli, on designs of Mantegna.

An helicoidal staircase leads to the first floor, where one enters the Entrance Hall. This part of the Castle was often rearranged towards the 15th century, in order to prepare the rooms of Isabella of Este. Half a century later, it was modified again by Giulio Romano on the occasion of the marriage of Federico II and Margherita Paleologo, the last heiress of Monferrato.

Here are the most beautiful rooms of the castle. Apart from the famous Room of the Married Couple, there are the Hall of the Lonely, which keeps a magnificent fireplace probably designed by Mantegna, the Middle Hall, the old bed-room of Isabella, the Cloaks Hall, with its ceiling decorated by stuccoes and grotesque figures, the Hall of the Grotto and Lady Paleologo's bath-rooms. A small staircase, called the Martyrs' Staircase, leads to the second floor, with the political prisons, where the Belfiore Martyrs were kept.

Having come back to the groundfloor by the Captain's staircase and again to the first floor by Aeneas staircase, after the majestic east loggia and the south one, one enters Isabella's Rooms. They were built in 1519, when Isabella became a window. Here we find the beautiful Secret Garden, the Small Study, well known for its wooden decorated ceiling, the Grotto, with fine tarsias, and the Big Hall, which keeps fine frescoes by Lorenzo Leombruno.

In the southern portico there are other rooms of Isabella Larger Apartment, with traces of old decorations, an interesting testimony of the refined cultural atmosphere, in which Isabela of Este lived. She was one of the most representative personages of the Italian Renaissance.

The Room of the Married Couple

Once called « Camera Picta », the Room of the Married Couple, as today it is usually called, was entirely frescoed by Andrea Mantegna, who displayed here all the treasures of his art, so celebrating the humanistic glory of the good prince Ludovico and his family.

Since January 1457 Mantegna, on Marquis Lodovico's proposal, had decided to come to Mantua as court painter. But it was only in 1460 that he left Padua, where he had become famous.

The great artist, who had a strong and difficult character, imposed himself on the others very soon. Mantegna's style spread very quickly — a style, so immediate and violent, in which the artist realized the graphic ideas concerning the most various works.

Unfortunately nothing remains of his first works made in Mantua. The large and complex decorations, which Mantegna made in the Gonzaga Palaces of Goito, Caviana and Mantua, have disappeared. The decoration of the chapel of St. George's Castle, too, went lost. It was one of the first and most important works he made by Marquis Lodovico's order.

Other paintings, which he probably made during the happy Mantuan period, when Mantegna created his most lyrical works, enrich today the most important museums in the world. The only work kept in the town is the wonderful decoration of the Rooms of the Married Couple, the most complex masterpiece of his artistic maturity. The experiences the artist had, when studying the classics and during his youth, when in Padua and Venice studied the great Tuscan artists, who had worked in Veneto, and those he had during his journeys in Tuscany in the period 1466-1467, all have flowed into this work.

The composition, which influenced also the contemporary architecture, represent the classical pavilion, with its vault covered with fake low-reliefs. In the centre there is a round piece of sky, which is one of the most known pictorial motifs of Renaissance. On the wall of the fireplace and on that on its left, are painted the two main episodes of the decoration, one representing « Marquis Lodovico's family gathered for a ceremony », probably the reading of the papal breve, by which the second-born son Francesco was made cardinal; and the other, « The Meeting of Marquis Lodovico with his son, cardinal Francesco and his retinue ».

Apart from their iconographical meaning, the poetical truth and the beauty of the works of the Room of the Married Couple, lie in the vivid language of Mantegna, the evocative power of his stories. In them the ideal world of the ancient classical forms and the inner history of the contemporary personages form the theme of a deep humanistic subject. In the « Camera Picta » we have a great picture of contemporary life, made by the author with originality, well knowing the relation of the painted part with the architectonic structure of the hall. On a high base, the walls open as if forming a large portico, beyond which there is the landscape. In this picture, Mantegna finds a monumental classicity, expressed in a large and luminous vision, with a narrative tone, simple and majestic at the same time.

Here is the scene where Mantegna has represented the Gonzaga Court. Marquis Lodovico sits down, enjoying a privileged position within his family, and speaks to his secretary, Marsilio Andreasi. Near him, a little lower, sits Barbara of Brandeburg, a learned and clever woman, who could take his husband's place when he was out, in leading the State and the family. Between the two princes there is the first son Federico, who in 1478 became the third marquis of Mantua. Before him there is the young Lodovico. A little below, almost submerged by her relatives' clothes, there is Paola, their youngest daughter.

Behind Barbara of Brandeburg there are the other two sons, the fourth-born son Rodolfo and Barbara, who married Eberarde, duke of Wurtemberg. The noble figure between those of Federico and Rodolfo, could be the mathematician Bartolomeo Manfredi or Francesco Bevilacqua, who succeeded Vittorio of Feltre in the education of the Marquis' sons, while the young man closing the scene on the right, perhaps is a noble relative of the family.

Lastly there is Nana, which Mantegna has described very realisticly and draws our attention. On the background there is a banister of coloured marbles, finely engraved with geometrical motifs, beyond which some flowered branches come out. This family portrait, made, according to some critics, in 1472-1474, reflect the new decorative sense of the artist, which reveals a serene contemplation of nature and man.

The photographs on these pages show us some details of the Court: Barbara Gongaza (on a side, above); Marquise Barbara of Brandeburg (below); Marquis Lodovico speaking to Marsilio Andreasi (above).

On the left wall of the hall is represented the meeting of Marquis Lodovico and his son Cardinal Francesco, in the presence of relatives and courtiers (side photo). In the centre of the scene there is the Cardinal, quite conscious of his importance and dignity. He had an exuberant and sensual nature, which at that time was considered normal even in churchmen. He was, however, a man of great culture, very fond of literature and art, and the pride of his family. Lodovico, his father, stands very reverently before him. Between them one can see also the profile of Gianfrancesco, the third-born son of the Gonzaga. At the right end there is Federico, the heir of the marquisate. In the scene there are again Lodovico, whose hand his brother cardinal holds, and Federico's two sons, the little Sigismondo, on the foreground, and, a little behind him, Francesco, the future marquis of Mantua, the husband of Isabella of Este. Lastly, on Federico's side, a little in the shadow, one can see the self-portrait of Mantegna himself.
In the photo above there is a detail of cardinal Francesco.

Lodovico Gonzaga was born in 1414 from Gianfrancesco and Paola Malatesta. In the photo above we can admire a detail of his head and face.

He had become marquis in 1444. Being a man of great culture, educated with his brothers by Vittorino of Feltre, he knew how to overcome the uncertainties and fears of his youth. He found serenity and balance ruling the life of his family and State with a strong hand. He helped the latter particularly with liberal and happy provisions, encouraging the most valid institutions and continuing to cultivate his own cultural interests. The prince looks here firm and quiet, a very wary person, both in his private and public life, a man who has nothing of that introvert and timid character of his green years.

In the photo on the side page there are the portraits of Francesco and Sigismondo Gonzaga, taken from the scene of the Meeting.

We can admire here the whole scene representing « The Meeting of Marquis Lodovico and his son, cardinal Francesco and his retinue », divided into two parts by the door, but representing the same subject. A classical dignity fills the scene, giving a aulic character to it. This fact, however, does not prevent us from distinguishing the various personages here represented. All this shows the refined capacity of Andrea Mantegna as portrait-painter.

In this scene, the landscape on the background is very suggestive. Mountains and hills extend far away, where the author has represented an ideal town with classical monuments, wrapped in an absolute silence.

Small white figures move, looking very busy, on the slopes of the mountain. On the left side there are the foot-men waiting. Here the landscape is even more fantastic, made as it is of steep rocks dominated by fortified towns, with massive walls and steep scaffoldings.

In the centre of the scene, above the door, there is the Latin epigraph supported by puttoes, concluding the artist's work: « For the most renowned Ludovico, second marquis of Mantua, a very good prince of unabated faith, and Barbara, his most renowned wife, incomparable glory of women; their Andrea Mantegna of Padua made this modest work in their honour, the year 1474 ». This epigraph bear witness to the affective nature of the relations between the painter and the Lords of Mantua, the town which, having given hospitality to Mantegna, had to keep the work, which represents the highest stage of his activity.

Above: a detail of the little Sigismondo Gongaza; on a side: a detail of the foot-men waiting. The scene of the meeting refers most probably to the year 1472, when the cardinal visited his native town, in order to begin the construction of the Basilica of St. Andrew, on designs of Leon Battista Alberti. During the summer of that year the prelate took the waters at Porretta. He called Mantegna there and told him many things about the monuments and ruins of Rome, so satisfying the artist's passion for archaelogy. The other scene of the gathered court must refer to the return of Francesco to Mantua. It seems then that a real historical link unites the two episodes, already harmoniously connected one to the other in this decorative composition.

The photographs on this page show us some details of the scene of the Meeting, the landscape spangled with the buildings of a mythical classic town, where, according to some authors, Mantegna represented ideally the city of Rome he had always dreamed to see and had not yet seen. The quiet atmosphere of this hilly landscape and the deep blue sky with white clouds rising from the flowered hedge of the hunting, reach undoubtedly lyrical heights.

On the side page there is the portrait of Andrea Mantegna appearing near Federico Gonzaga. This self-portrait shows him to us, as the archive papers describe him, that is solitary and moody, always frowning, but deeply grateful to the marquises of the town, in whose court the artist had found a new compositive balance in a humanistic, but informal environment.

Above there is a detail of the oculus of
the vault, where ladies and puttoes lean
out. The imaginary portico ends with a
ceiling with golden stuccoes, where in
the centre, in a new spatial and fascinating finction, the eye opens on the luminous sky. The individual architectonic elements of the whole converge here. It is
from here that the light flows on the
heads of the figures leaning out of the
banister. Here and there a small head ap-
pears among the openings of the balcony,
which confirm the perspective depth of
the scene.
The great decorative cycle of the Room
of the Married Couple, which represents
solemnly various aspects of the Gonzaga
court in a very ample composition, where
the poetical inspiration makes every cultural element adhere to reality and nature,
is one of the highest examples of the
art of Andrea Mantegna.
In the photo on the left: a detail of a
horse and a foot-man.
On the right: puttoes supporting the dedi-
catory epigraph.
On the large following plate there is a
suggestive image of the eye of the vault.

Near the royal palace of the Gonzaga there is the Cathedral, built centuries ago, but rebuilt in 1545 and the following years on designs of Giulio Romano. Of the preceding construction remain the Gothic right side and the Romanesque bell-tower dating back to the 12th century, with mullioned windows, while the cold Baroque-like facade dates back to 1757. It was made by Nicolò Baschiera. The interior, entirely re-made by Giulio Romano, is magnificent for its elegant lines and decorations. It looks like a palaeochristian basilica, but it is more sumptous, after the 16th century mannerism. The fourfold line of Corinthian columns with architraves, dividing the cathedral into five aisles, creates a suggestive play of shades and perspectives. On the outermost aisles there are the chapels once belonging to the various guilds of the town, adorned with fine frescoes, and stuccoed decorations.

Near the Cathedral there is a 15th century shrine, which can be reached by a passage. It is, the Chapel of the Crowned Madonna, probably made by Luca Fancelli. On the side page there is a detail of the scene of the Gonzaga Court, in the Room of the Married Couple.

The famous Pensile Garden on the Ducal Palace was built by order of Duke Guglielmo in 1579-1580. It is supported by a double order of archivolts and has an elegant pictorial decoration with leaves, made when the garden was built. The large Garden of the Rivers open on to it. It was made by order of Duke Guglielmo and used as court refectory.

On the side page we see, above, the Cathedral and the high Tower of the Cage, so called after the iron cage walled up in the middle of it, where at the Gonzaga's times the criminals were kept.

Below there is the solitary Castle Square, which originally was a courtyard of the palace. It was designed by Gian Battista Bertani in 1500. It is surrounded by porticoes on three sides, with a hemicycle in the central one, where there is an ancient entrance to St. George's Castle. From 1779 to 1785 the famous fairs of Mantua took place in this square, which can be reached by a long passage-way from Sordello Square.

In a small polygonal square, near Castle square there is the Palatine Basilica of St. Barbara, the court chapel of the Gonzaga, built by Bian Battista Bertani, by order of Guglielmo II, in the period 1552-1562.

The original belfry of the church, considered to be the most important one of the ducal buildings erected by Bertani, the vivid pre-Baroque pictorial effect of the facade and the luminous interior are expressions of the scenographic taste of the artist.

Of the many precious masterpieces the basilica once kept, today remain only two great paintings of Lorenzo Costa the Elder and the « Martyrdom of St. Barbara » by Brusasorci. In the sacristy there are a bronze crucifix attributed to Giambologna, a buckle by Cellini an da reliquary of St. Barbara.

Below there is the Exhibition Courtyard, made by Bertani, on which the balconies of the wonderful Exhibition Gallery open to.

On the side page, above, there is the Courtyard of Honour, surrounded by the halls of the New Gallery, where some paintings of the Museum's collection are exhibited, and by the sumptuous Hall of Mirrors.

In the photo below there is the Garden of the Pavillon, one of the many gardens of the palace, from where one can see the large and noble facade of the Domus Nova (New Housel), made by Luca Fancelli.

The Ducal Palace

The Magna Domus and the Captain's Palace, which rise on the east side of Sorbello Square, are the oldest facades of the so called Ducal Palace, which is not a single building, but consists of various architectonic structures. In order to understand how such a peculiar palace came to be as it is today, we must go back to the time when the Gonzaga family seized power. In 1328 they chose as their official residence the palaces built by Bonacolsi at the end of the 13th century, namely the Domus Magna and the Captain's Palace, which formed the first nucleus of the future ducal palace and later were called « Old Court ».

In the interior few halls keep a medieval look. We may mention the vast Armoury Hall and the Corridor of Passerino, with pictorial decorations, which date back to the early times of the Gonzaga rule.

During the following decades the Gonzaga family left the Old Court and went to live in more recent buildings. By some rearrangement works and the addition of new palaces, linked together by a net of covered passages, the palace became in the 17th century a true town in the town.

It was separated from the remaining part of the built-up area by walls and had within its perimeter, apart from the noble buildings, also many other subsidiary buildings, such as stores, houses for officials, guard-houses, and also streets, alleys and squares.

We can say that the palace of Mantua, variously structured as it is, does not look like the other Italian princely houses, but recalls to mind only the Vatican Palaces, which perhaps inspired the Gonzaga.

If we consider the long series of halls, this palace looks like a precious exhibition of rooms, most of which dating back to the 16th century or to the beginning of the 17th century. Some parts, however, have been decorated in the late 18th century, after the Gonzaga times. They are places such as the Hall of the Rivers, the Hall of Mirrors and the Apartment of Tapestries, which were rearranged by order of the Austrian Court, which succeeded the Gonzaga in the government of Mantua.

Since such 18th century artistic expressions bring us into a neo-classical atmosphere, it is clear that the Ducal Palace constitutes a great summary of the history of art in Mantua, from the Gothic ago to the neo-classical period.

Pisanello's Hall

Having reached the top of the staircase, which from the left side of the entrance hall, situated under the portico of the Captain's Palace, leads to the first floor, one enters the Hall of the Dukes, called also Hall of the Princes. It is so called because of the frescoed 18th century medallions placed all around it, and representing the personages of the Gonzaga family, who ruled the town.

In 1969, after a long and passionate research, some wide remains of an important decoration by Pisanello were found in this hall. Pisanello worked in Mantua for a long time and influenced all the artistic expressions. His influence can be seen in the refined elegance of the architecture, in the heraldic taste and in the subtle naturalism of the plastic works, which accompanied it. Antonio Pisanello, so called because he was born in Pisa, was a sumptuous court painter, a very clever and versatile designer. During his artistic education, he was influenced by Stefano of Verona, when he was in this town. Then he became the greatest disciple of Gentile of Fabriano. Pisanello had all the interests and the curiosity of a humanist. He studied the past, investigated nature and was a versatile technician.

All his work shows a deep attraction to the peculiar forms and aspects of the visible universe. Before such an universe, the artist did not take the impassive attitude of a scholar, but rather an attitude of curiosity, a genuinely poetical curiosity, which came out of the very heart of the late international Gothic culture, that is on a ground of a rarefied decadent lyricism.

Pisanello moved often from one court to the other. In Mantua he made perhaps one of his greatest works, namely the great decoration of the Hall of the Princes. It represents the deeds of Arthurian knights, in a vast landscape, and a bloody tournament probably referring the same legend, where the artist has represented personages of the Gonzaga court and various emblems and symbols of this family The cycle, which was made partly in sinopia and partly in fresco, does not look complete. In the photo below there is a detail of the bloody tournament: a dead warrior lying on the ground.

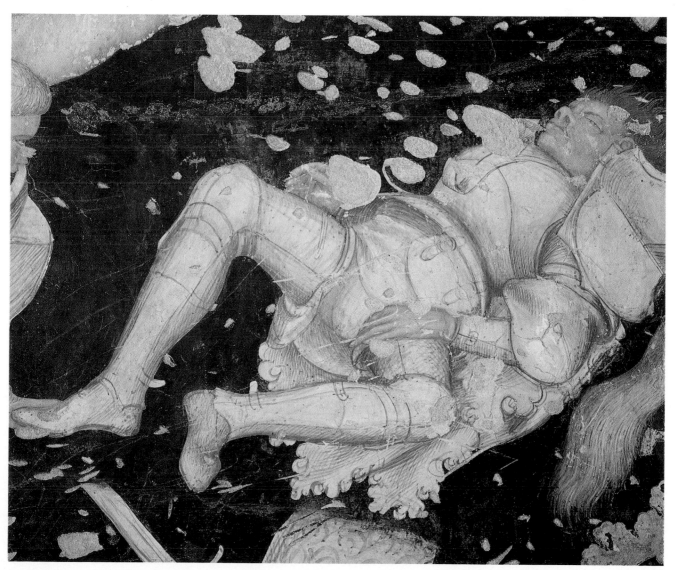

The pictures on this page show us other details of the decoration. This fantastic vision of a romantic chivalrous ideal met with success. It influenced the painting of the Po area very much. It is known that the contemporaries indicated the room so decorated as « Pisanello's Hall ». Some letters of Filippo Andreasi and Luca Fancelli addressed to Federico I Gongaza tell of the collapse of the ceiling of « Pisanello's Hall ».

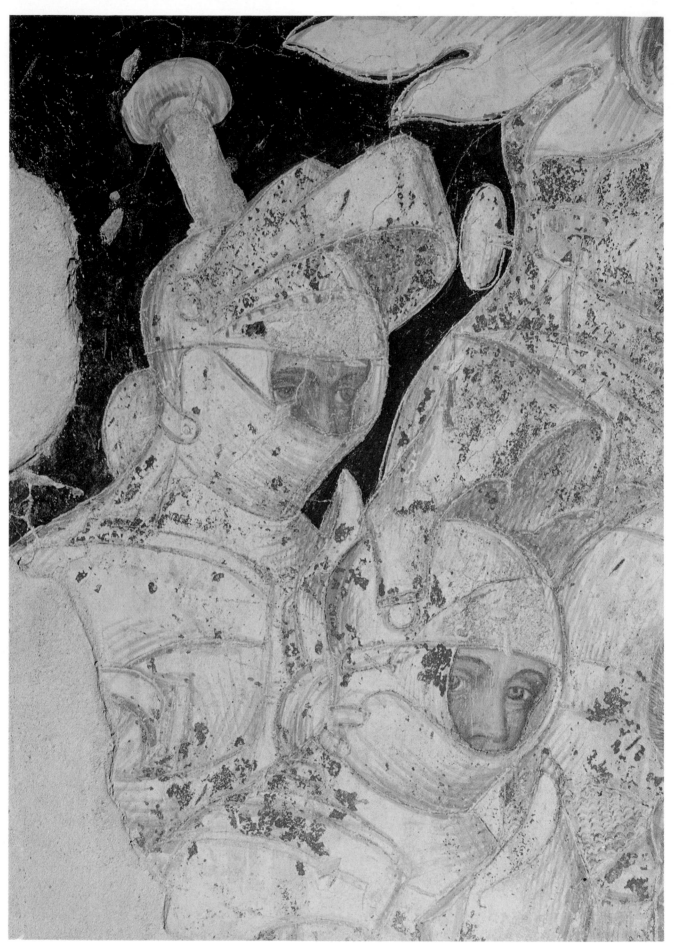

A group of warriors and the portrait of a woman are some other details of the great cycle, found by Paccagnini in this hall in 1969.

The peculiar character of his art, a court art meant for a small group of privileged people, and mainly the disappearance of his most important works, already at the time of Vasari, caused Pisanello to be forgotten after his death. Yet he influenced many contemporary painters and his research in the natural phenomena prepared the way for the studies made by Leonardo, in order to create a new scientific basis of the painting art — a Renaissance basis, we could say.

On the following pages: a wounded warrior kneeling.

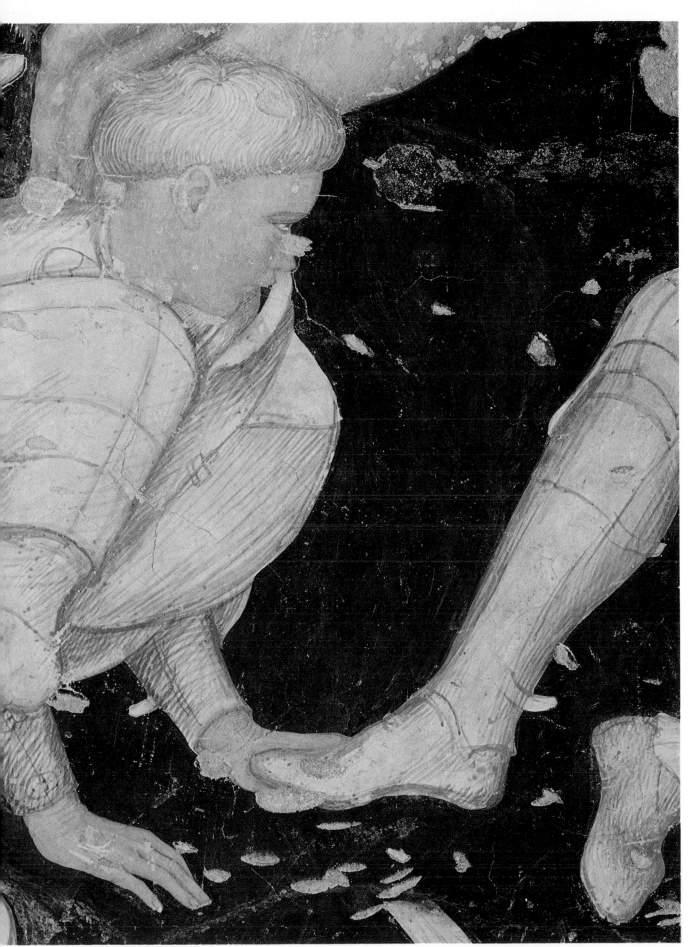

Once the remains of the decorative cycle were found (see other details in the pictures), the plaster of the frieze was completely detached, so recovering most of the frescoes and sinopias. Originally the decoration probably covered all the walls, but now only the upper part of them, because the lower one was completely demolished and remade at the beginning of the 19th century.

The work, made, according to most of the critics, between 1439-40 and 1443-44, taking into account the main documented contacts between Pisanello and the Gonzaga court, is thought to have been made, according to some other critics, during the period 1446-47, when the artist must have been in Mantua to coin the medals of Ludovico and Cecilia Gonzaga, to which the frescoes would be stilistically connected. On the other hand, it is less probable that he made this work in the period 1439-1444, since at that time Pisanello had been forbidden to enter Mantua. It does not seem possible that in such circumstances he could dedicate himself to a vast and exacting work, such as the frescoes of the Ducal Palace.

47

Valuable works of art and very important collections are kept in the various halls of the Ducal Palace.

In the Exhibition Gallery, which we see partly in the photo above, on the left, there are, among other works, the so called Virgil, of the 13th century Venetian school (below, on the left); the bust of Marquis Francesco II, attributed to Mantegna; the Fall of the Bonacolsi family, by Domenico Morone, signed and dated 1494 (photo above). The Gonzaga collection of Greek and Roman sculptures is very important. It is the richest one in Lombardy and includes Greek originals and Roman copies of Greek statues.

In the photo above there is a detail of the frescoes adorning the Hall of the Cloak, one of the most magnificent halls of the Palace. This hall, whose decorations, representing the foundation of the town and the beginnings of its life, recently have been attributed to Primaticcio, has been called after the mythical foundress of Mantua.

We see below a picture of the wonderful hall, and, on a side, another detail of the frescoes.

Above, on the right, there is the great painting of Rubens representing «The Dukes Guglielmo and Vincenzo Gonzaga with their duchesses Eleonora of Austria and Eleonora de' Medici, adoring the Most Holy Trinity ».

Below there is a corner of the Archers' Hall, so called because it was the antechamber of the Ducal Apartment guarded by archers.

The next large plate shows us a hall of the Apartment

of Tapestries, which was transformed into the present shape by the Veronese Paolo Pozzo, by order of the imperial court of Vienna. One of the oldest copies of the 9 tapestries, whose first series is kept in the Vatican, made in Flanders on designs of Raphael, had to be kept there. The subjects of the tapestries, which were bought around 1530 by cardinal Ercole Gongaza and donated to Duke Guglielmo, have been taken from the Gospels of Luke and John and from the Acts of the Apostles. They refer to the life of the saints Peter and Paul.

The Hall of the Labyrinth is part of the Ducal Apartment, built by order of Duke Guglielmo in the second half of the 16th century. It was rearranged and completed, at the time of Duke Vincenzo, by the architect Antonio Maria Viani between the end of the 16th century and the beginning of the 17th century. On a side, a foreshortning of the beautiful ceiling, where the labyrinth is represented, a motif very common during the Renaissance and particularly dear to the Gonzaga.

On the side page we see, above, the Hall of the Rivers, whose walls are decorated with personifications of the rivers of the Mantuan area. In the ceiling there is an Allegory in honour of the Empress Maria Teresa. The decorations were made in 1776 by G. Anselmi of Verona.

Below there is a detail of the Hall of the Mirrors, with frescoes made by local artists, under the direction of Viani, at the beginning of the 17th century, most of them, however, were re-painted in 1779, when the walls were decorated and adorned with mirrors. The decorations present mythological and allegorical figures.

Sordello square

The vast and majestic Sordello Square, so called after the Provencal speaking trombadour of Mantua, mentioned and loved by Dante, was the heart of the public, political, re-religious and artistic life of the town for many centuries. The monuments surrounding it have to be divided into two groups: the medieval palaces, built by Bonacolsi around 1300, severe and majestic brick structures with flat-topped battlements and ogival windows, and, in a corner of the square, the Cathedral and the Bishop's House, with 18th century facades. It is so that the various testimonies of the lively history of Mantua look at the symbols of the local ecclesiastical life.

On the left side of the beautiful square there are the Acerbi's Houses and the Bonacolsi Palace, now Castiglioni Palace, which keeps, in its rich archives, the autophaph of the « Courtier » by Baldassarre Castiglione. Beyond the nearby and suggestive Bonacolsi Alley, with fly-over and medieval houses, there is the Baroque Bishop's House.

The front side is closed by the Cathedral, while the right side is occupied by the two palaces forming the prospects of the Ducal Palace, the Magna Domus and the Capitain's Palace, where the Gonzaga family came to live, after they siezed power.

In this building they kept the political pivot of the State of Mantua during all their long domination, that is for almost four centuries.

After the fall of the dynasty, this famous square, too, began to decline as pulsating heart of the town.

The Herbs Square, with its old buildings and porticoes, under which there are many shops, the Gothic house of the merchant Bonacolsi, the huge dome of St. Andrew's silhouetted against the sky, dominating some small houses renewed during the neo-classical age, is one of the most coloured squares of Mantua, after Sordello Square.

On the eastern side of it there is the linear and powerful construction of the Palace of Reason (photo above), built in 1250 and restored in 1942. At the Gonzaga times it was the seat of the High Court of Justice and the notarial archives.

Near the Palace there is the Clock Tower, built in 1473 by Luca Fancelli. After the Tower, a little lower than the level of the square, there is St. Laurence's Rotunda

In the two pictures on the left side there are the staircase of the Palace of Reason and the monument to Virgil, which is in the Mayor's Palace, whose back facade closes the nodth-east end of the Herbs Square.

ST. LAURENCE'S ROTUNDA – A round Romanesque church, built by order of Countess Mathilda of Canossa towards the end of the 11th century. The interior of the church, of which we can admire some images on the preceding pages has one anular nave, created by 10 massive columns and covered by hemispheric dome.

ST. ANDREW'S CHURCH – The imposing and artistically important Basilica of St. Andrew, the best work of Leon Battista Alberti, is certainly the greatest temple of the town.

It was rebuilt, from its foundations, on a preexisting church, since 1472, on designs of Alberti and under the direction of Luca Fancelli, who worked at it for about twenty years, building the facade and the front body. The basilica was completed in two stages, between 1597-1600 and 1697-1699. The large and elegant Baroque dome was added by Filippo Iuvara sometime between 1732 and 1782.

On the left side of the original facade, where Alberti left the schemes followed in the medieval churches and re-elaborated the architectonic idea of the Roman Triumphal arches there is the wonderful Gothic belfry (1413) of the preceding church. The classical vestibule leads into the magnificent interior of the temple. It is Latin-cross shaped, with one powerful nave, covered by a barrel-vault, flanked alternatively with square chapels and small chapels with domes. Andrea Mantegna was buried in the first small chapel on the left side of the nave. What is amazing in this church is that the various elements added in later periods, such as the dome or the pictorial decorations of the interior composed sometime between the 16th century and the end of the 18th century, do not alter the austere form of the Albertian spirit.

Having left the small Andrea Mantegna Square, where the Basilica of St. Andrew is, and crossed Guglielmo Marconi Square, and gone along the characteristic Corso Umberto I, adorned both with Renaissance porticoes, whose capitals are variously shaped, one reaches Felice Cavallotti Square. Here is the Social Theatre, built by the architect Luigi Canonica between 1818 and 1822, when it was inaugurated.

It has a Ionic pronaos and a very elegant interior. It is one of the most characteristic neo-classical Italian theatres.

From Cavallotti Square starts Corso Vittorio Emanuele, at the end of which, near the All Saints Church, once there was Pradella Gate, which closed the town to the west. Outside the Gate, in an area now full of buildings, there extends the Belfiore Valley, where between 1851 and 1853 ten patriots, fighting for national freedom, were killed. A simple monument recalls the sad event.

On a side: a stretch of Via Roma.
Below we can admire the stage of the Scientific Theatre. Near Broletto and Herbs Squares, which formed the political centre of Mantua in the 13th century, there is the centre of the studies gravitating on the quiet small square dedicated to Dante. Around it there are the most important cultural buildings of the town, namely the State Archives, a vast and precious depot of documents, whose most important part is constituted by the Gonzaga archives; the magnificent 18th century palace, once the seat of the Jesuits' University, now the Town Library; and The Palace of the Virgilian Academy, designed by Piermarini in 1773.
On the groundfloor of the building there is the Scientific Theatre, so called because it is attached to the Science and Literature Department of the Academy.
This theatre, a very beautiful construction by Antonio Bibiena, was built in 1769 for concerts and conferences. It has four orders of boxes and a fixed scene.
On the following plate: another sight of the interior of the theatre.

The Rio, of which the photo shows a foreshortening in one of the most picturesque corners of the old town, is a canal, built perhaps at the end of the 12th century, connecting the Upper Lake to the Lower Lake, crossing the town.
On the side page, above, there the Belfiore Martyrs Square.
Below there is the monument to Virgil, by the architect Luca Beltrami. It was inaugurated in 1927. It is adorned with a big bronze statue of the poet, made by Emilio Quadrelli.
On its sides, two groups represent the heroic and pastoral poetries.
The monument rises in the vast Virgilian Square, once occupied by a unhealthy marsch. Since the 18th century the place was reclaimed and the construction of the square began. It was completed only in the following century, when the first monument in honour of the great poet was erected. Later on, it was dismantled and then replaced with the present one.

A panoramic sight from the « Mincio Boat-club ».

The Sordi Palace, built in 1680 by the Flemish architect Francis Geffels, is one of the oldest and most sumptuous houses of the Mantuan aristocracy. The monumental courtyard (photo above) and the large staircase are adorned with statues and stuccoes by G.B. Barberini. Above, on the left, we see Andrea Mantegna's House, with the foundation date, 1476, engraved in an angular marble. Perhaps this house was designed by the artist himself and restored in our century. It was often rearranged and spoiled. It presents, however, its original cubic structure, in which a small cylindrical courtyard is harmoniously inserted. Not far from Mantegna's House, there is the church of St. Sebastian, designed by Leon Battista Alberti in 1460. The temple, which is the first example of the Renaissance building art, is Greek-cross shaped. Unfortunately in 1925 it suffered, in the outside and in the interior, an absurd restoration, which altered it noticeably. Today it is a sanctuary dedicated to the Fallen for the Homeland.

In the photo below, there is Rigoletto's House.

Having gone out of Mantua by the Mills Bridge, the dam dividing the Upper Lake from the Middle Lake, going on beyond the village of Cittadella, where is the Giulia Gate designed by Giulio Romano, by the state road leading to Brescia, one reaches the Fountain Wood. This wood is crossed by canals and symmetrical avenues ending in lay-bies and dominated by green elms, oaks, ash-trees, turkey oaks and poplars.

The wood, a preserve of the Gonzaga, dating back to the 14th century, reached its greatest extension during the Renaissance, when it extended from the Marmirolo area to Goito. At the end of the 16th century, Duke Vincenzo built there a small castle and transformed the wood into a sort of pleasureground, with beautiful kiosks and fountains. At the end of the Gonzaga rule, it was abandoned and partly demolished. Today the wood extends for about 228 hectares, with a perimeter of about 7 kilometres. In a bare patch there is the house, built by Viani, with cylindrical corner towers and a monumental entrance (photo below, on the left).

Not far from Cittadella of Mantua, there are the remains of Favorita, the sumptuous villa built by order of Duke Ferdinando between 1615 and 1624, by the architect Nicolò Sebregondi. In spite of the ravages it suffered, the building is still monumental. Perhaps Gonzaga wanted to establish the seat of his court in it (photo above, on the left).

The Tea Palace

Immediately out of the ancient Pusterla Gate there is one of the most magnificent Renaissance villas in Italy, the most significant monument made by Giulio Fomano. It is the Tea Palace, whose name comes from that of a place once called, according to some, Tejet in dialect (where the small cut of the grass takes place), according to others, field of Teio, the last Ostrogothic king, who camped here; according to others, it was called « teieto », that is a village of huts. It was built by order of Marquis Federico II Gonzaga, near the stables of the favourite horses.

Giulio Romano worked at this construction and the successive decorations for ten years, from 1525 to 1535. Raphael's disciple was helped by a group of painters, sculptors, carvers and decorators, who worked always under his direction. Perhaps they simply realized the various works to be made in the building on designs of their master. Among them there were Gian Francesco Penni, Rinaldo Mantovano, Primaticcio, Benedetto Pagni, Gian Battista Scultori, Fermo of Caravaggio, Girolamo of Pontremoli and Nicolò of Milano.

The low palace extends on a square area, with a central courtyard and a very large back garden, closed by exedra, built later on. The architecture, made of Doric and natural elements, was certainly suggested by the intention of creating a harmony with the natural environment, which provided its background. It represented in Northern Italy, also with its play of symbols and eccentricities, the influence of the new tendencies, by which in Rome the mannerism had begun to show its first signs.

In this building, where architecture and decoration match each other so well as to create an expression of art very allusive and made of antinomies, Giulio shows more clearly then elsewhere the anti-classical nature of his spirit. Though today one usually enters the building from the side facing the town, originally the official entrance was that still existing on the west side, where the atrium looks like that Antonio da Sangallo Junior had built a few years earlier in the Farnese Palace in Rome.

In the courtyard, the motif of the falling triglyphs, which interrupt the trabeation with a strange rhythm, seems to be the most significant symbol of all the art of Giulio Romano.

On a side: one of the monumental wings of the building (above)
On the next plate: the Entrance of Honour of the Palace.

The Hall of Psyche

Giulio Pippi, called Romano, had been the most important disciple and collaborator of Raphael till the master's death in 1520. He was then the artist who more aptly than others could realize the ambitious ideas of Federico II. The young marquis during the three years spent at the papal court of Julius II, between 1510 and 1513, had been influenced by the modern taste created in Rome by Raphael's school.

Giulio moved to Mantua at the end of 1524 and gained, with his first works, the immediate favour of Federico. Very quickly he succeeded in obtaining such a privileged position that he could controll and direct the urban and architectonic development of the town and all the artistic production of his time.

The richness and variety of the works produced by Pippi during his uniterrupted activity from 1524 to his death in 1546, and his « so many designs of chapels, houses, gardens and facades » transformed so much the city-centre that, according to Vasari, tha town was « all charming and pleasant » and had the look of a « new Rome ».

Apart from his easel works, Giulio Romano projected and erected public and private buildings, transformed and restored already exsting buildings, in which he could express the various aspects of his personality as architect, decorator and scenographer. But where the fantasy of this artist could express itself most was in the realization of the Tea Palace, built, as we have said, by order of Federico II. The marquis had certainly in mind the worderful suburban villas he admired in Rome, when he charged Giulio with the construction and decoration of this sumptuous house, dedicated to his princely amusements and particularly to his love-affair with Isabella Boschetto.

As in the beautiful Roman villas, where the artist had worked before he came to Mantua, the structure of the Tea Palace was projected in harmony with « the nature of the place», picturesquely animated in the facades by a fake rusticated ashlar, which gives the construction the look of a building « not walled but truely born ». The ideal centre of the Palaces is the precious Hall of Psyche, whose paintings develope the subject of Love by the famous mythical fable taken from the Golden Donkey by Apuleius, and dear to the Renaisance fantasy. Below, a detail of the decoration.

A detail of the Hall of Psyche. The frescoes of the Hall of Psyche belong to the first stage of decorations, made between 1527 and 1530, while a second stage, ending with the spectacular scenographic effect of the Giants Hall, took place between 1530 and 1535. The frescoes cover the upper part of the walls, with a wonderful combination of decoration and architecture. Between the walls and the vault runs the inscription « Federicus Gonzaga II Mar. V.S.R.E. et Reip. Flor. Capitaneus Generalis honest ocio post labores ad reparandam virt. quieti construi mandavit » (Frederick II Gonzaga, fifth marquis, general captain of the Holy Roman Church and the Florentine Republic, in order to rest after work and restore his energies in peace, ordered it to be built).

THE HALL OF PSYCHE – Details – According to some, Giulio Romano intended to represent here and exalt marquis Federico's love for Isabella Boschetto, a love which had aroused the wrath of Isabella of Este. Others think that the artist represented here allegorically the ascent of the soul (Psyche) from the prison of matter to the high domain of spirit, having overcome obstacles and sufferings. But apart from the inspiring theme, the beauty of this hall lies in the chromatic vividness of the decorations, in the endless richness of the decorative and pictorial motifs, in the restless intellectual research of a harmony between the classical world and the Christian world, in the interesting landscapes on the background.

The two walls without windows are occupied by the great composition representing the wedding banquet of Cupid and Psyche, with the intervention of the gods (side photo). On the other two walls, the bath of Venus and Mars (photo above) and other two mythological scenes.

Together with Giulio Romano, Rinaldo Mantovano, Pagni, Fattore, Luca of Faenza and Fermo of Caravaggio worked in this hall. The presence of different artists has not altered the formal unity of the decoration, thanks to the continual intervention of Giulio in the works, for which he provided the designs his collaborators had to use when working at the walls entrusted to them.

We see here other scenes taken from the great pictorial cycle of the large hall of Psyche. We find here that element of a subtle paganism, which is at the basis of the formal conception of the Tea Palace.

From the Hall of Psyche we get into the Horses Hall, which is the largest one of the palace and was the large entrance to the banquets. The sumptuous ceiling we see on the side page, rests on a frieze of puttoes and leaves. It has painted and golden lacunars, where rose-windows and the symbols of Mount Olympus and Salamander alternate. The decorations of the hall, so projected by Giuio Romano, were made by Rinaldo Mantovano, Benedetto Pagni and probably also by another of Giulio's collaborators.

THE HORSES HALL – Six wonderful portraits of horses belonging to the races bred by Federico Gonzaga. They were made by Rinaldo Mantovano and dominate the Hall called after them. The walls are decorated with architectonic elements, figures of pagan deities and scenes representing the labours of Hercules.

THE ZODIAC HALL – The vault is divided by hexagons and quadrangles, in which figures of gods, the Months, the Signs of the Zodiac are frescoed. The medallions on the walls above, represent the events of the human life in connection with the astral influences. They were painted by Giulio Romano, Rinaldo and Pagni. The fireplace and the frame, too, made by Andrea de' Conti and Nicolò of Milano, are quite precious.

PHAETON'S HALL — This hall, adorned with a fine decoration, was once the bed-room of the Gonzaga. The central octagon of the vault, representing the fall of Phaeton, was frescoed by Giulio Romano. The other paintings, developing also a mythological subject, were made by the same artists who worked at the Zodiac Hall. The stuccoes by Primaticcio and the marble fireplace are quite beautiful.

CAESAR'S HALL — The frescoes of this hall, made by Giulio Romano, Primaticcio and Pagni, represent the Story of Julius Caesar. In the middle of the vaut there is Caesar who has Pompey' letters burnt. The frieze with puttoes is a neo-classical remaking.

THE GIANTS HALL, the most spectacular room in the Palace. The walls merge into the vault through the fresco of the « Fall of the Giants struck down by Jupiter», made by Rinaldo Mantovano an other collaborators, on cartoons of Giulio Romano. All the decorations of this hall, with huge and impressing figures, develope the theme of Power, with flattering references to the emperor Charles V, who in 1530 had given Federico II the title of Duke

GIANTS HALL – Details

THE HALL OF STUCCOES – In this hall, the stuccoed frieze, with two orders, running all along it and made by Primaticcio and G.B. Scultori in 1531, is wonderful, indeed. The decoration representing a Roman triumph, celebrates the coming of Charles V to Mantua in 1531.

On the side page, above, there is the Cottage of the Grotto, an isolated and almost hidden building, a secluded place within the Palace, as the Palace itself had been conceived as a secluded place compared to the town.

The building includes an octagonal vestibule, decorated with grotesque figures, Attilius Regulus Hall, with paintings probably by Rinaldo Mantovano, a small loggia decorated by Agostino of Mozzanega and Girolamo of Pontremoli, and the secret garden with lunettes by Primaticcio.

Of the grotto at the end of the garden, only the structure and traces of a decoration remain.

Below there is the large luminous loggia of the Tea Palace, which opens on to the courtyard of honour and divides the halls of the buildings into two groups, or main apartments.

The museum of D'Arco Palace

The D'Arco palace, that opens on to D'Arco Square with its solemn neo-classical facade, includes various architectonic bodies, apart from a beautiful garden and a courtyard. The front body, till the exedra, was built in 1784 and during the following years by the architect Antonio Colonna that, specially in the lines of the facade, was inspired by Palladio's art.

The building was owned by the Counts of D'Arco of Trent, who since 1740 had partly settled in Mantua, where they had inherited the Counts Chieppo's house. In 1780 Giovan Battista Gherardo D'Arco charged Antonio Colonna with the complete rebuilding of the preexisting palace. One century later, another member of that family, Count Francesco Antonio D'Arco, bought, from the marquises Dalla Valle, the area situated beyond the exedra and including some Renaissance buildings, and the garden, so enlarging the old residence of the Chieppo family.

More recently the palace that keeps furniture, paintings and other objects of great artistic value, has been transformed into a public museum according to the will of Giovanna of the Counts D'Arco.

The first hall we meet, in the interior of the building, is that of the Ancestors, so called because in it are kept 60 portraits, all executed between the 16th and the 18th centuries, once were in Trent and later were transferred to Mantua.

From the Ancestors Hall one gets into the other halls. On the left side there are the rooms that in the last century formed the private quarters of the owners of the palace; on the left side there are Halls of the picture-gallery.

On the right side we find the hall of the architectonic perspectives, adorned with elegant neo-classical decorations and furniture dating back partly to the 18th century and partly to the first half of the 19th century; the Portraits Hall, with 18th century furniture and many paintings representing ladies and gentlemen from the late 16th century to the first half of the 19th century; the Still Life Hall, that once was the dining-room and keeps a table laid with 18th century crockery; the little Loggia, a very beautiful room adorned with fine decorations and various sculptures; the Music hall, where a collection of musical instruments is kept.

From the Ancestors Hall, turning to the left, we get into the Picture-gallery that includes seven halls.

The first hall is Diana's Room, so named after the representations on the vault. Very interesting are a painting of Caravaggio's school representing Joseph and Potiphar's wife, the figure of a satyre, attributed to Bartolomeo Manfredi of Cremona, a painting representing "Juno, Ceres and Psyche", by Sante peranda of Venice, "The rich man's supper", executed in the 16th century, and a painting of the Caracci's school of Bologna, representing "Jupiter and Antiope".

Then comes the Red Hall, a typical example of aristocratic room of the second half of the 19th century. Here are furniture, paintings and wonderful objects of porcelain and silver. In the middle of the hall there is the portrait of Count Francesco Antonio D'Arco, by whose order all the furniture of this room was made.

Then we enter Pallas Hall. Its lacunar ceiling is very beautiful; in the middle there is the image of wisdom, after which the hall is named. On the walls there are some 16th-17th-18th centuries paintings, mostly portraits. Noteworthy are the portrait of a lady dressed in black, attributed to Girolamo Forabosco, the image of a friar, by Jacob Denys, a Fleming; the portrait of Vincent I Gonzaga, the duke of Mantua, and an old copy of the portrait of baldassar Castiglione, executed by Raphael and today kept in the Louvre Museum. Some portraits of ladies are extremely beautiful.

18th century furniture and 16th-17th centuries Flemish paintings adorn the Green Hall or Hall of Justice, where is also a fine work dating back to the second half of the 15th century and representing the "Madonna with the Child and Angels".

Near it there is the Neo-classical Hall, adorned with stuccoes and neo-classical knick-knacks.

From the Green Hall one gets into the Hall of the Sacred Representations, where mostly religious paintings are kept. The furniture dates back to the 17th and 18th centuries. Among the may works here kept, noteworthy are: "Christ bearing the cross", executed in the 16th century, attributed to Maineri, "St. Jerome" by Bartolomeo Montagna; a "Deposition" by Rubens' school; "Christs's Scouring" by Lorenzo Costa the Younger;

"Christ ascending to Heaven", attributed to Lorenzo Lotto; a fine "Crucifix" by Van Dick's school; a "Madonna" by the 16th century Umbrian school; "Christ bearing the cross", attributed to Sodoma (16th century).

Then come the Passage of the Reliquaries, where each case keeps a fine collection of reliquaries, and the Hall of Alexander the Great or Bazzani Hall. This hall is so named after the seven large paintings representing episodes of the life of Alexander the Great. These paintings, by Giuseppe Bazzani of Mantua (18th century), represent from right to left: Alexander while receiving the mother of Darius, the King of Persia; Alexander with his horse Bucephalus; Alexander with soothsayers; Alexander with Darius' family; Alexander at the death-bed of Darius' wife; Alexander the Great meets its future wife, Roxana; Alexander's and Roxana's wedding.

In the same hall there are some Renaissance and 18th century works.

As we have already said, behind the main body of the palace, beyond the garden, there are other architectonic bodies, among which the most interesting one is what remains of a building dating back to the end of the 15th century. There are some rooms of the original construction, namely three rooms on the ground floor and a very large one on the upper floor.

Now we get into the ground floor, where are two halls and a chapel.

The first hall present pensile capitals and amphoras of the Roman period; it keeps also religious paintings and the genealogical tree of the Agnelli family of Mantua.

In the second hall there are some painting, among wich one by Giovan Battista Venanti (16th century), representing the Magi visiting the Child Jesus. Two small tables support some 17th century niches.

A door, surmounted by a painting by Cignaroli, with Madonna, the Child and Saints, leads into the Chapel that keeps a 17th century marble altar, a beautiful altar-frontal of Morocco leather, and ancient vestiments.

On the upper floor of the building there is the large Hall of the Zodiac, that we can admire in the lower picture.

The Hall of the Zodiac, all adorned with frescoes, is a wonderful example of humanistic culture. The pictorial work, executed around the year 1520 by Giovan Maria Falconetto of Verona, is inspired by the theme of the Zodiac, hence the name of the hall. It illustrates myths and legends concerning the constellations. The walls are divided into twelve panels separated by pillars and surmounted by friezes. Each panel represents a sign of the Zodiac. The paintings represent also ancient buildings of various Italian towns, such as the Coliseum in Rome, Theodoric's Mausoleum and the church of St. Vital in Ravenna.

A panel, exactly that of the Libra, was destroyed in the 17th century, when the large fire-place, situated at the end of the hall, was built. Near it there is an iron case with its lid lifted up to let the visitors se its lock, which is truly extraordinary for its ingenuity.

From the hall of the Zodiac we get dow again into the garden, and from here into the kitchen built in the 19th century. Copper, brass and pewter cooking vessels are kept, all in good order, in this kitchen.

In all the museum, after all, all the furniture, paintings and other objects are situated in the same rooms and in the same places as before the death of Joan D'Arco.

Hall of the Zodiac

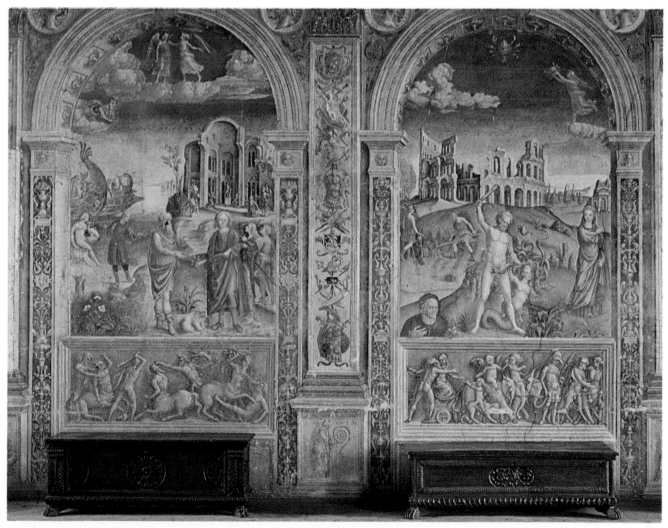

The Sanctuary of the Madonna of Graces

A few kilometres from Mantua, in the village called « Le Grazie » (Graces), there is the Sanctuary of the Madonna of Graces. The cult of the Madonna of Graces dates back to the early Middle Ages. This cult was begun by fishermen and countrymen of Mantua, grateful to the Virgin Mother for avoided dangers.

The Madonna was venerated in a rough image on a capital rising on the right side of the Mincio, at 7 kilometres from the town. When the veneration of the people of Mantua for the Madonna increased, the church built between 1150 and 1200 became too small to receive the crowds of pilgrims. It was so that around 1400 Francesco Gongaza, when Mantua was delivered from pestilence, had the present sanctuary built in Gothic-Lombard style, on designs of Bartolino of Novara.

The facade, adoned with windows, brick cornices and spires, is preceded by a long portico, with round arches and lunettes frescoed in the 16th and 17th centuries, and has a beautiful Renaissance portal.

The interior, which we can admire on the next large plate, has only one nave with slender ribbed cross-vaults, whose partitions are frescoed with 15th century floreal motifs. The Renaissance apse and presbytery are simply wonderful.

Towards the end of the 16th century, the characteristic wooden superstructure with niches was added. The niches contain votive wooden, stuccoed and waxed statues, representing more or less famous personages, who are supposed to have received favours. On the left wall the Mantuan warriors taking part in the battle of Pavia, are represented.

The sanctuary went through a period of true glory and artistic splendour. Princes and noble families made gold and silver offerings; warriors, who had received favours, left here their arms, all precious examples of medieval rarities; famous artists made very important works for the sanctuary. Later on, however, time and wars damaged the temple, which only since the middle of the 19th century was renewed thanks to loving care of the bishops of Mantua and the renewed veneration of the faithful.

Among the works kept in the sanctuary, quite interesting are the 17th century temple-shaped Tabernacle, the « Madonna of Graces », a painting of a venetian 15th century unknown artist, which glows near the monumental main altar, two beautiful anconas by Lorenzo Costa Junior, representing the « Assumption » and the « Martyrdom of St. Laurence », two « Assumptions » by Giuseppe Bazzani, an ancona, «St. Sebastian » by Francesco Bonsignori. We may mention also the mausoleum of Baldassarre Castiglione, designed by Giulio Romano, and that of Camillo Castiglione, his son, who died in 1598, and the « Martyrdom of St. Hippolytus » by Lattanzio Gambara.

Villimpenta

Villimpenta situated along the right side of the river Tione, is an important agricultural centre of the province of Mantua. It keeps, as many other nearby towns, picturesque remains of medieval fortifications. At first it belonged to Verona; since 1391 to the Gonzaga domain.

On an islet on the shores of the Tione, there is the castle of the Scaligeri, mentioned in documents since 1047, and forming, with the strongholds of Goito, Castiglione Mantovano, Castelbelforte, Ostiglia and Quistello, a strong defensive line between the Mincio and the Po. Of the imposing pentagonal building remain two polygonal towers and a massive corner tower, 35 metres high, with a stripe of corbels on the upper part.

Near the castle, we can see in the pictures on these pages and on the next one, there is Villa Zani, built by order of the Gonzaga perhaps in 1530 and representing clear Giulianesque lines.

The villa has elegant porticoes in the centre and is surmounted by a high garret. Quite original is the interior, where a large central hall leads into the various rooms. In the central square of Villimpenta there is the parish church of St. Michael, with a Baroque facade and a belfry dating back to 1673. Paintings dating back to the 12th and 18th centuries and a tabernacle adorned with small statues, made by F. Maderno and Gabrieli, are kept in it.

Many other places of the province of Mantua are very interesting. For the visitor who wishes to complete his knowledge of Mantua with that of its environs, we may mention Pietole, rather Pietole Vecchia, which, according to well founded tradition dating back to the Middle Ages, is the ancient Andes, Virgil's birth-place. Then there is also Goito, where Sordello was born at the beginning of the 18th century; Solferino, where a terrible battle took place during the Italian Risorgimento. Then there are Ostiglia, Castel d'Ario, Castiglione delle Stiviere and many other places, rich in works of art and historical memories concerning mainly the Gonzaga family. We should not forget that some side branches of the great dynasty conquered, between the 14th and the 16th centuries, at the borders of the Mantuan territory, some lands which were independent of the mother-town, so transforming small villages into mini-capital towns, which went through periods of real splendour.

Sabbioneta

Sabbioneta is the richest monumental centre of the whole province, so much so that it is called « Little Athens ». The town was founded in the second half of the 16th century by Vespasiano Gonzaga, an ambitious prince, belonging to one of the side branches of the great family.

Having inherited some suburban lands of the province of Mantua, including the small village of Sabbioneta, he decided to destroy the latter and to built a small ideal town, conceived by him according to the criteria of a humanistic rationality and later realized according to the aesthetic late-Renaissance taste.

Even today Sabbioneta presents itself mainly as the work of Vespasiano, whose strong personality it reflects. His was a genuinely Italian personality, enriched by his many journeys in various European countries and by the political and cultural contacts he had in Spain.

The town is surrounded by star-shaped walls and consists of a net of quiet streets meeting at right angle, with an elegant square, on which the main church and the Ducal Palace open to. Very interesting are also the other ancient buildings of Sabbioneta, in which the various halls follow one another with numerous decorations, made mainly by Lombard and Emilian artists.

Sabbioneta has also buildings posterior to the age of his founder, showing so that the life given to it by Vespasiano, went on for some time after his death. These buildings are gentlemen's houses, 17th century churches, a synagoge, which recalls the existence of an Jewish community, which, under the protection of the prince, led a remarkable cultural life.

The town represents, therefore, the best example of a refined 16th century ducal seat. Its name recalls the idea of sand. And perhaps a bare sandy place must have been that where the town rose. The town is said to have been called so after St. Sabino, who preached in these places. But more probably its name comes from the nature of the soil. The fact remains that Sabbioneta is a very ancient town. It was a Roman station during the imperial period, as many findings clearly show. Vespasiano made it a splendid court, where he gathered the most famous men, writers and artists of his times. At his death, since he had no direct heirs, the town, which in 1577 had the ducal title, became the feud of many families, till 1748 when it was annexed to Austria.

Below there is Victory Gate, which opens, with the Imperial Gate, on the perimeter of the walls.

In the centre of the Castle Square, the ancient drill-ground, there is a Roman column, with bronze base and capital, made by Andrea Cavalli (1584). The column is surmounted by a statue of Pallas, perhaps coming from the sack of Rome, which took place in 1527. On a side we see the Imperial Gate (above) and Garibaldi Square (below), once called Ducal Square, with the Ducal Palace, the Parish Church and other elegant buildings.

On the next plate we have a view of the interior of the Olympic Theatre or Ancient Theatre, an elegant building erected on designs of Vincenzo Scamozzi, who considered it his masterpiece. This rectangular theatre, with a fixed scene demolished in the last century and replaced by a platform, was the first covered theatre built from its foundations. Modern restorations have brought to light the frescoes of a Venetian school, once adorning its walls.

Above there is the Olympic Theatre, with a facade in pure classical style, very elegant in its architectonic lines and finishs.

The Garden Palace, also called Summer Palace, of which we can admire here the entrance-hall with elegant vaults with lacunars, if outwardly looks like a simple house with two floors, in the interior shows all the magnificence, because of which the duke love to spend here his free days. It was begun in 1568. It consists of a series of rooms decorated with refined frescoes developing mythological or Roman subjects, stuccoes and grotesque figures, all faithful expressions of Vespasiano's personal taste.

The pictures us two details of the Hall or Myths (above), adorned with a double stuccoed frieze and a pavilion vault representing the exploits of the Gonzaga and the myths of Philira and Saturn, Aracnes, Icarus, Marsia and Phoeton, frescoed by Bernardino Campi; and of the Aeneas Hall (below), decorated with friezes and low-reliefs with golden stuccoes, by Fornaretto and with some frescoes by Campi, representing scenes of Aeneid.

The Palace, embellished on the outside by a rich cornice sculptured in oak wood, takes its name from the back garden. It presents on the right side a passage once communicating with the castle and demolished in 1794. It led directly into the armoury hall. The Cabinet of Graces, of which we have a detail of the decoration on the left, was frescoed with grotesque figures by Fornaretto, and adorned with elegant stuccoed vaults. Behind the Ducal Palace, a solid two-storied building erected in 1568 on designs of P. and B. Tusardi, there is the high octagonal building of the Gonzaga church of the Crowned Madonna, in a small quiet square. Here is also the magnificent mausoleum of Vespasiano Gonzaga, made by G. B. della Porta (1592). Above the sarcophagus there is the ancona, where, between Justice and Force, there is the wonderful statue of the prince and duke of Sabbioneta, a true masterpiece of sculture.
In the dome-shaped interior, large arches form representations of saints, and prespective backgrounds create a peculiar scenographic effect.

On the right side of the Castle Square there is the Gallery of the Ancients. It is a long and imposing brick building with a portico with 26 arches, to which correspond as many closed arches on the upper floor. It was erected in 1583-84 and presents walls frescoed by Pietro Martire Presenti and Giovanni and Cherubino Alberti, and a beautiful wooden ceiling.

This Gallery, where Vespasiano had gathered many masterpieces, among which marble busts, Roman and Greek statues and low-reliefs, taken by Rodomonte during the sack of Rome and later transferred to Mantua in 1774 by order of Mary Therese of Austria, is a real triumph of the painting art, which recalls to mind the papal court and that of the kings of France, both well known for their splendour.

In the photo above there is a detail of the Horses Hall. The next plate shows us another beautiful picture of the Gallery.

Revere

Revere, the ancient Riperium, was long ago an islet emerging from the waters continually fed by the floods of the Po.

Little by little it became dry land, though keeping a certain strategic importance, so much so that the people of Mantua, Reggio and Modena always contended for it. The Modenese, having seized it, built there a castle, which the Mantuans set on fire.

The German emperor gave the village to the bishops of Mantua, who, on their turn, gave it to the Gonzaga.

It was Ludovico Gonzaga that in 1450 built that Ducal Palace, which today is the seat of the Municipality of Revere. Of the pre-existing castle, only a tower remains.

Two Etruscan necropolis, situated 10 kilometres far apart, have been found in the area. Revere, situated on the left side of the Po, has an elegant Baroque church, the parish church of the Annunciation, with a beautiful curved facade dating back to 1750-1776 (photo below on the side page).

The interior, with only one nave, keeps frescoes by Giuseppe Milani of Parma, two paintings by Giuseppe Bazzani, the « Madonna and St. Clare », the « Annunciation », and a 16th century terra-cotta representing a Madonna with the Child.

In the side photo we can admire the Ducal Palace, begun by Luca Fancelli in 1450, and presenting elements reflecting the styles of Brunelleschi and Michelozzo, and even a certain medieval influence. This squared palace, made of bricks, represent one of the most interesting moments of the beginnings of the Renaissance in the Po area. It has a magnificent marble portal and a beautiful courtyard surrounded on three sides by a portico with columns. The right wing of the building houses the Museum of the Po, where collections of archaelogical, artistic and historical material bear witness to the history of the various civilizations which followed one another along the banks of the river.

The photo below shows us a view of the town, seen from the banks of the Po.

S. Benedetto Po

This town, founded in the 11th century and lying not far from the banks of the Po, gravitated around the ancient Benedictine monastery, after which it was called. It seems that this monastery dates back to the 10th century.

Its territories increased thanks to successive donations, specially from the Canossa family.

Very important is the basilica of St. Benedict (photo above), rising in the middle of what remains of the Abbey of Polirone, one of the most important Benedictine centres, so called because it was built between the Po and the Lirone, a river where the larger river flows into. It was foundd in 1007, when a Romanesque structure rose. Later on, the buildings of the convent were added to it. The whole structure was variously transformed through the centuries. The church, dominated by the high cuspidated belfry, presents today the facade made by Giulio Romano between 1544 and 1547.

The interior, too, with a nave and two aisles, was rearranged and decorated in 1500. Of the original Romanesque structure it keeps only the columns near the presbytery.

In the basilica, very interesting are the choir with wooden stalls dating back to the second half of the 16th century, and the cloister (photo on the side page).

Pieve di Cavriana

Not far from Cavriana, an ancient hunting resort of the Gonzaga, who built there a castle, today an important wine centre, the beautiful Romanesque church of « Santa Maria della Pieve » rises on a hill. It was built in the early 12th century and modified in the 17th century. The facade of the church, which we can admire on the large plate on the preceding pages, the three apses, of which the middle one has been rebuilt (photo above), and the sides (side photo) are crossed by pilaster strips ending with small arches. The slender cuspidated belfry is embodied into the building.

The interior keeps remains of frescoes made in the 12th and 14th centuries, and a Gothic statue of the Madonna of Mercy, perhaps dating back to the 14th century.

Pieve di Coriano

The parish church of the Assumption is the ancient church of Coriano, built in bricks in 1082-1085, and restored at the beginning of this century. It has a facade divided into thre parts, crossed by semi-columns, decorated on the upper part with arches, and a very suggestive interior, with truss roof and frescoes dating back to the 14th and 15th centuries. Not far from the church of Coriano, one meets another interesting Romanesque church, namely that of the village of Ghisione.

INDEX

Photographs: Plurigraf
APT Mantova - Toni Lodigiani pag. 20 - 21 - 24 - 95 - 97b

© Copyright by CASA EDITRICE PLURIGRAF
S.S. Flaminia, km 90 - 05035 NARNI - TERNI - ITALIA
Tel. 0744 / 715946 - Fax 0744 / 722540 - (Italy country code: +39)
All rights reserved. No Part of this publication may be reproduced.
Printed: 1997 - PLURIGRAF S.p.A. - NARNI

L. 12.000
I.V.A. INCLUSA